THE FIRST HISTORY BOOK YOU'LL WANT TO READ!

JOEY NOVICK   NEIL BERLINER
MICHAEL MORSE   RON BEAU PHILLIPS

ILLUSTRATIONS MICHAEL MORSE • MIKE CRUMBS

Best
Neil

Editors

Alex Berliner

Neil Berliner

Grant Moore

JANUARY

January 1

1914: The St. Petersburg-Tampa Airport Line becomes the world's first scheduled airline. This also marks the first time that a passenger with a Group Four ticket gets up and stands at the gate as soon as boarding for Group One is announced.

January 2

1860: Urban La Verrier discovers the planet Vulcan. Although he never directly observes it, observations of the planet's star make its existence only logical.

January 3

1953: Frances Bolton and her son, Oliver, become the first mother and son to serve simultaneously in the U.S. Congress. This led to some problems, however, as Oliver would often not be allowed to vote on a bill because he hadn't finished his vegetables.

January 4

1970: The Beatles complete their very last recording session together. Or, as Yoko Ono puts it, "Mission Accomplished."

January 5

1975: At 8 P.M., the musical "The Wiz" opens on Broadway. At the 9:15 intermission, hundreds of audience members simultaneously take "a wiz".

January 6

1838: First public demonstration of a telegraph by Samuel Morse and Alfred Vail. Historians are not sure whether it was a takeout order for Italian or Chinese, but all agree that the restaurant got it wrong.

January 7

1984: Two-time Cy Young Award winner Denny McLain is indicted on drug trafficking, embezzlement, and racketeering charges. On the bright side, he becomes the leader in wins, ERA, and strikeouts in his prison softball league.

January 8

1889: Computer pioneer Herman Hollerith patents his punched card calculator, paving the way for the eventual creation of a vast global network of misinformation, rude comments, and cat videos.

January 9

1570: Tsar Ivan the Terrible launches the Massacre of Novgorod, killing 15,000 people. Survivors of the massacre dub him, Tsar "Actually Not That Bad Compared to What Hitler's Gonna Be Like Some Day".

January 10

1954: Jerry Lee Lewis' "Great Balls of Fire" hits the UK pop charts. The next morning, Lewis awakens with an "unusual burning sensation" upon urinating, and calls a urologist.

January 11

2002: The first prisoners arrive at Guantanamo Bay. The Yelp reviews are brutal.

January 12

1959: Record company Motown is founded by Berry Gordy Jr. as Tamla Records, thus beginning an American tradition of white people dancing very badly to very good music.

January 13

1978: NASA selects its first American women astronauts. They endure a rigorous interview process, but no, there was no "space suit competition".

January 14

1699: Massachusetts holds a day of fasting for wrongly persecuting "witches". The following day, they resume eating witches again.

January 15

2021: Leonardo da Vinci's painting "Salvatore Mundi" becomes the most expensive painting of all time, selling for $450.3 million U.S. The purchaser is thrilled to learn that also included in the purchase price is a coupon for a beautiful frame at any Michael's location.

January 16

1962: Shooting begins on "Dr. No", the first James Bond film. Yes, his enemies have been trying to shoot 007 ever since.

January 17

1994: A devastating 6.6 earthquake hits Los Angeles, marking the first time that town is interested in something that's less than a seven.

January 18

1997: Boerge Ousland of Norway becomes the first person to cross Antarctica alone. His route is so desolate that he passes only three Starbucks along his trek.

January 19

1937: Howard Hughes flies from Los Angeles to New York in a record 7 hours and 22 minutes. When asked why he did it Hughes replied, "Have you ever tried to get real pastrami in L.A.?"

January 20

1945: Franklin D. Roosevelt is sworn in for an unprecedented fourth presidential term. He winds up serving for 4,422 days, or, in modern-day terms, 402 Scaramuccis.

January 21

1988: Bob Dylan is inducted into the Rock & Roll Hall of Fame. His acceptance speech is translated into five languages including English.

January 22

2018: Netflix becomes the largest digital media and entertainment company in the world, worth $100 billion. Co-founders Ted Sarandos and Reed Hastings definitely "Netflix and chill" that night.

January 23

1978: Sweden becomes the first nation in the world to ban aerosol sprays. Tourism to the country drops dramatically when Trip Advisor issues a nationwide body odor alert.

January 24

1984: The Apple Macintosh computer goes on sale. This date would forever be remembered not only by tech geeks, but also by everyone who didn't buy Apple stock at thirteen cents a share.

January 25

1979: The first case of a robot killing a person in the U.S. occurs when one comes home unexpectedly and catches his human wife in bed with a toaster.

January 26

1926: John Logie Baird gives the first public demonstration of television in his London laboratory. Within minutes, those witnessing this technological miracle get fidgety and ask him to "see if there's something better on another channel."

January 27

2018: IKEA founder Ingvar Kamprad dies. His funeral is postponed several days, as family members have difficulty putting together his coffin with that little Allen wrench.

January 28

1958: A patent was granted to the LEGO company for their toy building blocks, leading to decades of playtime delight for children and eternal agony for parents' feet.

January 29

1594: Mathematician John Napier proves that the world will end in 1688 or 1700. He was always better at social studies than math.

January 30

1947: The town of Yerba Buena (meaning "good plant") is renamed San Francisco (meaning "What schmuck would build a city in a place with hills like these?").

January 31

1990: The first McDonald's is opened in Russia, and uses a KGB-inspired slogan "You deserve a break today for criticizing the government... would you prefer your arm or your leg, comrade?"

FEBRUARY

February 1

1992: Barry Bonds signs the highest single year contract in MLB history, $4.7 million with the Pittsburgh Pirates. The achievement makes Bonds swell with pride. As do the dozens of performance enhancing drugs he's taking at the time.

February 2

2004: Janet Jackson exposes her boob during the Super Bowl halftime show, upsetting millions of viewers who tuned into the game expecting to see wholesome family entertainment and chronic brain injuries.

February 3

1995: American astronaut Eileen Collins becomes the first woman to pilot a space shuttle. To achieve this, Collins has to endure rigorous academic training, strenuous physical testing, and male astronauts mansplaining which pedal is the gas and which pedal is the brakes.

February 4

2004: The Web site Facebook is launched, finally giving people around the world the opportunity to see how stupid everybody's else's opinion is.

February 5

2014: National Shower With A Friend Day is created to promote water conservation and to take the public's mind off the much-less-enthusiastically-received National Shower With A Stranger Day.

February 6

2019: Researchers from RMIT University in Australia say that honeybees are able to add, subtract, and understand the concept of zero, but are unable to understand the words, "OW, OW, STOP STINGING ME!"

February 7

1976: The game Monopoly goes on sale, and within hours, the phrase "Why do I have to be the thimble?" is uttered for the first time by a human being.

February 8

1974: 34-year-old Ringo Starr releases the song "You're Sixteen, You're Beautiful, And You're Mine" as a single in the UK and, amazingly, no investigation is launched.

February 9

1825: John Quincy Adams, son of 2nd President John Adams, is elected commander-in-chief by the House of Representatives, beginning the long-standing tradition of denying blatant political nepotism in the U.S.

February 10

2021: A planetoid named Farfarout is confirmed as the most distant object orbiting the sun, according to the astronomer who named the planetoid, Professor William Ilovemakingbadjokes.

February 11

1650: French philosopher Rene Descartes dies; he stops thinking and, therefore, stops amming.

February 12

1941: The first injection of penicillin into a patient occurs at Radcliffe Infirmary in Oxford, England. How brave is that patient to agree to the treatment after hearing the doctor say, "We're going to inject this stuff we made from mold into your body!"?

February 13

1866: Jesse James holds up his first bank, the Clay County Saving Association in Liberty, Missouri. He got $15,000 and seven of those pens with the little chains on them.

February 14

1982: "Night of 100 Stars" takes place at New York City's Radio City Music Hall. Although, since Danny DeVito is one of the performers, it really should have been called "Night of 99 ½ Stars."

February 15

1842: The first adhesive postage stamps are made available in the United States. This news is enthusiastically received by the 19th century sexually repressed public, who are delighted to be finally allowed to lick something.

February 16

1937: DuPont chemist Wallace Hume Carothers patents nylon. Carothers died before he could be put on trial for his contribution to the popularity of the unsightly 1980's fashion fad, parachute pants.

February 17

1883: A man named Ashwell patents the "Vacant/Engaged" toilet lock in London, England. Look folks, not every invention is the electric light bulb. Give the guy a break; at least now you don't have some idiot pounding on the door while you're trying to drop a deuce in peace.

February 18

1979: The first "Antique Road Show" is broadcast. A man who came to watch the show with his 89 year-old grandmother is devastated when he's told that she's worth only eleven dollars.

February 19

1910: Typhoid Mary is freed from her forced isolation and goes on to cause several more outbreaks of typhoid in the New York area. People throughout New York finally realize that they probably shouldn't hang out with someone named Typhoid Mary.

February 20

1872: The Metropolitan Museum of Art opens in New York City, allowing school children to take a field trip to see wealthy people's tax write-offs.

February 21

1989: Pete Rose meets with baseball Commissioner Peter Ueberroth to discuss Rose's gambling. The meeting quickly deteriorates when Pete asks his odds of getting into the Hall of Fame before he croaks.

February 22

1987: Andy Warhol dies after being famous for 13,400,000 minutes.

February 23

1988: Lights are installed in Wrigley Field, enabling the Chicago Cubs to play night games. After finishing the season twenty four games out of first place, the entire Cubs roster becomes terrified, as their maniacal fans can now identify the players by their faces.

February 24

1989: Stalker Margaret Ray is found in David Letterman's home, claiming to be his wife. She is immediately arrested and crowned the winner of Letterman's 'Stupid Human Tricks' segment.

February 25

1862: The First Legal Tender Act of 1862 is passed by the US Congress. This authorizes the first flat paper money as legal tender, thus making it much, much easier to tip strippers.

February 26

1991: The world's first web browser is presented to the public. This also marks the first time the words "find free porn" are typed into a computer.

February 27

1907: Sigmund Freud and Carl Jung meet for the first time. The meeting lasts 50 minutes, at which time they compliment each other on their "breakthrough" and hand each other a bill and appointment card for the following week.

February 28

1939: The erroneous word "Dord" is discovered in Webster's Dictionary. The publishers promise to launch an investigation and find out who was responsible for such a bleahgnak.

February 29

1960: The first Playboy Club, where men could emulate Playboy publisher Hugh Hefner and cavort with young women dressed in bunny costumes, opens. The club's success and expansion around the country is responsible for an uptick in sales of pipes, velvet robes, and penicillin.

MARCH

March 1

1692: The Salem Witch Trials begin in Salem, Massachusetts. No visual record of the trial exists, because all of the court sketch artists were turned into frogs.

March 2

1127: The assassination of Charles the Good occurs in Belgium, who, during the assassination, briefly becomes Charles the Good and Pissed Off.

March 3

1873: The US Congress enacts the Comstock Law, making it illegal to send any "obscene, lewd, or lascivious" book through the mail. Thankfully, they did not enact the Transparent Envelopes Only Law.

March 4

1793: George Washington gives the shortest presidential inaugural speech at 133 words. Some say this is because Washington was a man of action, not words. Others say it's because he forgot to sand down his wooden teeth and has a mouthful of splinters.

March 5

1971: Led Zeppelin play their eight-minute "Stairway To Heaven" live for the first time at Ulster Hall, Belfast. Out of habit, all radio deejays in attendance get up and take a bathroom break.

March 6

1869: Dmitri Mendeleev presents the first Periodic Table of the Elements. A century later, fans of TV's "Superman" try in vain to get Kryptonite added to the Table.

March 7

1876: Alexander Graham Bell is granted a patent for the telephone. He called the patent office to confirm, but was on hold until late 1877.

March 8

2008: President George W. Bush vetoes a bill that would prohibit the CIA from waterboarding and, on the off chance that Tony Hawk is ever interrogated, skateboarding.

March 9

1959: The Barbie doll is introduced at a Toy Fair in New York City. It took only moments for a group of construction worker dolls to start making catcalls at her.

March 10

1876: Alexander Graham Bell makes the first telephone call to Thomas Watson, saying, "Watson, come here. I need you." To which Watson replies, "New phone, who dis?"

March 11

408: The Goths lay siege to Rome. The entire city is soon awash in eye liner and black hair dye.

March 12

1951: By a vote of nine to seven, Baseball Commissioner Happy Chandler loses his fight to stay in office. Might want to rethink that nickname, Hap.

March 13

2020: Bill Gates leaves the Microsoft board after founding the company four decades prior. Gates explains he is leaving the company in order to "spend more time with his billions."

March 14

1794: Eli Whitney is granted a patent for the cotton gin. Investors become enraged when they learn that it doesn't turn cotton into gin.

March 15

44 BC: Julius Caesar is stabbed to death by several Roman senators, including Brutus, more than 60 times. The senate police describe the death as "probable suicide, move along now, nothing to see here".

March 16

1751: "The Father of the Constitution" James Madison was born to parents Nelly Conway Madison and "The Father of James Madison."

March 17

1950: Scientists at U.C. Berkeley create a new radioactive element. They inform the press that it's unstable, drains an enormous amount of energy, and rapidly decays. They therefore name it "californium".

March 18

1965: Soviet cosmonaut Aleksei Leonov becomes the first man to walk in space. He later admits that the experience was so terrifying that he sputniked in his pants.

March 19

1822: Boston is incorporated as a city, with the newly-formed city council making their first order of business to declare the official Boston motto to be "The Yankees Suck."

March 20

2020: American country music singer Kenny Rogers dies, proving once and for all that he does indeed know when to fold them.

March 21

2006: Jack Dorsey sends the world's first Twitter message. In retrospect, this is equivalent to Typhoid Mary's first coughing fit in public.

March 22

1895: Auguste and Louis Lumiere first demonstrate motion pictures using celluloid film in Paris. The event is marred by several patrons who refuse to turn off their telegraph machines during the movie.

March 23

1775: Patrick Henry delivers the well-known speech featuring the phrase "give me liberty or give me death," at the second Virginia Convention. The impact of this speech is lessened when people realize that Henry uses this phrasing constantly. For example, at lunch he would often exclaim, "Give me a chicken salad sandwich or give me death."

March 24

1883: The first telephone call between New York and Chicago is made, sparking the first interstate argument over whose pizza is better.

March 25

2019: A British Airways flight flies from London to Scotland instead of to Germany due to having an incorrect flight pattern. When questioned about the incident, the pilot asked, "Don't you ever get a sudden, irresistible urge to listen to bagpipes while eating Haggis and wearing a kilt? No?... Just me?"

March 26

1991: Sharon Osbourne leaves the popular TV show, "The Talk". Her husband Ozzy, however, renews his contract with "The Mumble".

March 27

1931: Leo Bentley of Lorain, Ohio bowled three perfect 300 games in a row. When asked later how he did it, he said, "I was in a rush that day. I had no time to spare."

March 28

1799: New York State abolishes slavery. It eventually comes back when someone coins the term "unpaid intern".

March 29

2010: At 1,109 feet, the Tokyo Skytree Tower becomes the tallest structure in Japan. The building immediately becomes the #1 goal on Godzilla's bucket list.

March 30

1964: The game show Jeopardy! premieres. Sorry, "What is the game show Jeopardy! Premieres?"

March 31

1916: the Dutch government ended all military engagements. Since then, all smitten Dutch soldiers and their sweethearts have had to run away and elope.

APRIL

April 1

1889: The first dishwashing machine is marketed. Millions of husbands say, "I already have a dishwashing machine: her!" That night throughout the U.S., adult male visits to emergency rooms increase by 45%.

April 2

1992: Mafia boss John Gotti is found guilty of five murders, conspiracy to murder, loansharking, illegal gambling, obstruction of justice, bribery, and tax evasion. Legal experts say he had more charges than a Kardashian with a new credit card.

April 3

1973: The first handheld mobile telephone call was made by an employee of Motorola, thus ushering in a new dark era where spouses coming home late can't claim they didn't call because they couldn't find a pay phone.

April 4

1860: The Pony Express begins its 1,800 mile route between St. Joseph, Missouri, and Sacramento, California. China's effort to emulate this mail delivery system, fails miserably and eventually turns into a restaurant chain: Panda Express.

April 5

2018: National Read A Road Map Day is created, a day every bit as relevant to today's youth as National Churn Your Own Butter Day.

April 6

2016: A baby is born with the DNA from three parents, thanks to genetic engineering. Upon hearing the news, TV host Maury Povitch reportedly suffers a mental breakdown and resigns.

April 7

1954: U.S. president Dwight Eisenhower voices fear about a "Domino effect" of Communism in Indo-China. Good, why should we be the only people eating that garbage?

April 8

1766: U.S. patent granted for the first fire escape. It was a wicker basket on a pulley and chain. A previous patent request for a "fire escape" had been denied decades earlier when some guy tried to patent "running away".

April 9

1962: President John F. Kennedy throws out the first ball at Washington's new DC Stadium. The Senators score four times, the Tigers score one time, and JFK scores twice with a couple of female concession workers.

April 10

1849: The safety pin is patented by Walter Hunt, who sells the rights for $400.00. So Hunt ends up getting stuck anyway...

April 11

1901: Construction of the Empire State Building is complete. The structure was built in accordance with the strict safety codes of New York City except for, ironically, the installation of a huge gorilla trap.

April 12

1892: George C. Blickensderfer patents the portable typewriter, finally allowing writers to be able to procrastinate outside their homes.

April 13

1999: "Suicide Doctor" Jack Kervorkian is sentenced to 10 to 25 years in prison for second-degree murder. Had he been given the death penalty, it would have opened the possibility to witnessing the first DIY execution in history.

April 14

1865: Abraham Lincoln is shot and mortally wounded by John Wilkes Booth in Ford's Theater in Washington, D.C. The incident would remain the worst thing to happen inside a theater until the years on end of Andrea McArdle terrorizing audiences night after night with her rendition of "*Tomorrow*" in "*Annie*".

April 15

1955: Ray Kroc opens the first McDonald's fast food restaurant in Des Plaines, Illinois. Kroc's first stroke of business genius is deciding not to name it "Kroc's."

April 16

2012: For the first time since 1977, no Pulitzer Prize is awarded for Fiction. True story.

April 17

1860: A 42-round bare-knuckle boxing match in England between Tom Sayers and John Heenan lasts two hours, twenty-seven minutes. The only way for someone in this century to experience that much pain and anguish for 2 ½ hours is to watch *The Godfather III*.

April 18

1963: Talk show host Conan O'Brien is born in Brookline, Massachusetts. Within hours, O'Brien is unceremoniously removed from the nursery and replaced with 13-year-old Jay Leno.

April 19

1971: Charles Manson is sentenced to life in prison. The sentence is literally the only thing Manson isn't crazy about.

April 20

1759: Composer George Frideric Handel is buried in Westminster Abbey, London. The coffin has only one Handel.

April 21

1986: Geraldo Rivera opens Al Capone's vault on live TV and finds nothing. Three years later, comedian Jerry Seinfeld makes a show about the discovery that becomes a big hit.

April 22

1056: The Crab Nebula, a supernova in the constellation of Taurus 6,523 light years from Earth, is last seen by the naked eye. But that is decidedly not the last time the words "crab" and "naked" are used in a sentence, usually followed by a trip to the local drug store.

April 23

1977: Dr. Allen Bussey completes a record 20,302 yo-yo loops. Immediately upon attaining the record, his parents react, "For THIS we put him through medical school?"

April 24

1908: Mr. and Mrs. Jacob Murdock leave Los Angeles on their way to becoming the first people to travel across the US by car. Mr. Murdock also becomes the first man to refuse to ask for directions in four different time zones.

April 25

1792: Nicholas Pelletier became the first person to be executed by guillotine. He tells his executioner, "Yo, if this thing doesn't work, heads are gonna roll! Oh wait, they'll also roll if it does work! My bad, bro! Later!"

April 26

1564: William Shakespeare is born. He continues to be until, in 1616, he is not to be.

April 27

1667: A blind and impoverished John Milton sells the copyright of "Paradise Lost" for 10 pounds. More like "Royalties Lost," am I right, folks?

April 28

2019: The TV series "Game of Thrones: The Long Night" episode debuts with the longest battle ever screened (nearly 80 minutes). Married couples everywhere shrug and say, "Eh, we've had longer."

April 29

1852: The first edition of Peter Roget's Thesaurus was published. Critics want to lambast the book, but can't think of the right words.

April 30

2015: NASA's Messenger space probe crashes into the surface of Mercury, causing widespread panic throughout the agency that their insurance premiums will go up.

MAY

May 1

1889: George Eastman begins selling his Kodak flexible rolled film for the first time. When nobody buys it, he realizes that he needs to invent a camera in which it fits.

May 2

1536: Anne Boleyn is arrested and imprisoned in the Tower of London, where she is eventually beheaded. Her only regret is that Yelp hasn't been invented yet so she can give the Tower one star.

May 3

2021: Bill Gates and his wife Melinda announce their divorce after 27 years of marriage. The next morning, their names appear at the top of the "Most Handsome Men" and "Most Gorgeous Women" in the World lists.

May 4

1932: Al Capone, convicted of tax evasion, enters the federal penitentiary in Atlanta. His incarceration served as a warning to future would-be gangsters... If you're going to murder, steal, extort, and intimidate, remember to keep all your receipts.

May 5

1904: Cy Young pitches the first perfect game in "modern" baseball history as the Boston Americans beat the Philadelphia Athletics, 3-0. Although one of the greatest pitchers of all time, he unfortunately never goes on to win a Cy Young Award.

May 6

1626: Dutch colonist Peter Minuit organizes the purchase of Manhattan Island from Native Americans for $24 worth of beads and trinkets. It would have been $20, but his Groupon had expired.

May 7

1867: Swedish chemist Alfred Nobel patents dynamite, the first of three patents he would receive for the explosive material. To boost sales, he immediately gets on the horn to hire celebrity spokesman Jimmy "JJ" Walker.

May 8

1979: The Cure drops their debut album "Three Imaginary Boys". They are approached to go on tour by metal band Poison.

May 9

1914: President Woodrow Wilson proclaims Mother's Day. Mothers around the country say, "Um yeah, brunch and flowers are great, but how about giving us the damn vote?"

May 10

1963: Decca Records signs The Rolling Stones on the advice of Beatle George Harrison. To Mick Jagger's great satisfaction.

May 11

1904: Surreal artist Salvador Dali is born in Figueres, Spain. The time of his birth is uncertain though, because it's very difficult to accurately read a melting clock.

May 12

1963: Bob Dylan walks out of The Ed Sullivan Show over a dispute about his song choice. The incident probably could have been avoided if there had been an English interpreter for Dylan on set.

May 13

1767: 11-year-old Wolfgang Amadeus Mozart's first opera, "Apollo et Hyacinthus," premieres in Salzburg, Austria. It was met with favorable reviews from music lovers and cries of "Why can't you write an opera?" from jealous parents with normal children.

May 14

1853: Gail Borden patents his process for condensed milk. Dairy lovers who'd previously had no room for milk rejoice.

May 15

1948: Israel declares itself independent, but still gets calls from its mother asking why it never visits.

May 16

1911: Remains of a Neanderthal are found on the Isle of Jersey. This is not to be confused with the thousands of Neanderthals found at the Jersey shore every summer.

May 17

1970: An anonymous buyer purchases ruby slippers worn by Judy Garland in The Wizard of Oz for $15,000 at auction, but immediately donates them to the Smithsonian Institute. The lesson here? Always keep the receipt in case something you buy doesn't fit.

May 18

2001: 101-year-old Harold Stilson becomes the oldest golfer to record a hole-in-one. It's the only time a centenarian enjoys hearing the phrase, "That was a great stroke!"

May 19

1926: Thomas Edison speaks on the radio for the first time, as host of the drive-time show "The Morning Zoo with Tommy F and The Weasel."

May 20

1992: American rapper Tung Twista raps 597 syllables in under 60 seconds. Problems arise when the Starbucks barista asks him to please repeat his order.

May 21

1999: All My Children star Susan Lucci finally wins a Daytime Emmy after being nominated 19 times, the longest period of unsuccessful nominations in television history. It's almost like her life is a soap opera.

May 22

1943: Pitcher Tommy John is born. A natural childbirth; no "Tommy John surgery" required.

May 23

1929: The first talking cartoon of Mickey Mouse is released. That means audiences have been waiting nearly 100 years for Mickey to reach puberty so his annoying voice changes.

May 24

1978: Management consultant Marilyn Loden first coins the term "glass ceiling" to describe invisible career barriers for women. Unfortunately, many misogynist male businessmen mistakenly think this is a suggestion for a way to allow them to look up the skirts of women working on the floor above them.

May 25

1992: Jay Leno becomes the permanent host of The Tonight Show, beating out David Letterman by a chin.

May 26

1967: The Beatles' *Sgt. Pepper's Lonely Hearts Club Band* is released. Young people listen to the psychedelic sounds of the groundbreaking album non-stop, as their parents yell through closed bedroom doors, "What's that funny smell coming from in there?"

May 27

1961: The first black light is sold, paving the way for hotel guests to find out exactly how disgusting their rooms really are.

May 28

1959: Two monkeys named Able and Baker travel 300 miles into space on the Jupiter space mission. While Able handled his newfound fame admirably, Baker became insufferable and entitled, actually forcing his entourage to peel his bananas and fling his poop for him.

May 29

1987: Pop star Michael Jackson attempts to buy The Elephant Man's remains. Amazingly, this isn't ever close to the weirdest thing he will do.

May 30

1890: First baseman Dave Foutz of the Brooklyn Bridegrooms hits the first home run ever during a doubleheader. The feat is even more impressive considering Foutz was wearing an ill-fitting rented tuxedo.

May 31

2005: Former FBI agent Mark Felt admits that he was Deep Throat in the 1970's Watergate scandal. Suspicions are initially raised when witnesses see him eating an entire hot dog without taking a bite.

JUNE

June 1

1938: The first issue of Action Comics featuring Superman is published. Exactly one week later, thousands of copies of it are thrown out by mothers across America, "until you stop getting C's and D's in everything!".

June 2

1851: Maine becomes the first state to prohibit alcohol. Maine bar owners try to convince customers to "Just have a nice refreshing iced tea" and all declare bankruptcy within a week.

June 3

2019: Jay-Z is named the world's first billionaire rapper by Forbes magazine, reducing his Problems down to 98.

June 4

2003: Martha Stewart is indicted on nine criminal counts stemming from her involvement in the ImClone stock scandal. She immediately begins working on a prison shank that can double as bottle opener and paté spreader.

June 5

2002: Dee Dee Ramone, bassist for the rock group The Ramones, dies. His funeral lasts exactly two minutes with no guitar or drum solos.

June 6

1934: President Franklin Roosevelt signs the Securities Act of 1933 - 1934, which leads to greater transparency and less fraud and manipulation when buying and selling stocks. Members of Congress cheer, saying "Well, at least he left in some fraud and manipulation!

June 7

1993: Singer Prince celebrates his birthday by changing his name to an unpronounceable symbol. Ironically, the symbol is always drawn correctly on his Starbucks cup.

June 8

1969: Guitarist Brian Jones is asked to leave The Rolling Stones. You know you have a bad substance abuse problem when you're kicked out of a band that has Keith Richards in it.

June 9

1906: National League baseball team the Boston Beaneaters end a 19-game hitting streak by beating the Cardinals 6 – 3. The person you have to feel sorry for is the Cardinals' catcher, who had to squat waist-high behind the Beaneaters for nine innings.

June 10

1692: Bridget Bishop is burned in the first Salem Witch Trial. She emphatically denies being a witch... "Bitch, maybe. Witch? No way! Hey, who do I have to turn into a frog before they rev up the AC in here? Is it just me?"

June 11

1979: Rock and roll legend Chuck Berry pleads guilty to income tax evasion and is sentenced to four months in prison. While incarcerated, Berry pens the little-known song "Chuckie B. Badd."

June 12

1987: U.S. president Ronald Reagan challenges Soviet premier Mikhail Gorbachev to, "tear down this wall". He continues, "In fact, tear down all the walls! Make Germany a completely "open floor plan" country!"

June 13

1957: An exact replica of the original Mayflower arrives in Plymouth, Massachusetts after a 55-day journey from England. Native Americans happening upon the event are heard to utter, "Oh shit, not again!"

June 14

1951: The U.S. Census Bureau dedicates UNIVAC, the first commercially produced electronic digital computer in the United States. It takes up 15,000 feet, employs 17,000 vacuum tubes, and is programmed by plugging and replugging some 6,000 switches, which makes it very difficult to use at home in your living room while watching television.

June 15

1924: Ford manufactures its ten millionth automobile as enthusiasts continue to be divided between "Ford men" and "horse men".

June 16

1963: Soviet Cosmonaut Valentina Tereshkova becomes the first woman to travel into space, orbing Earth 48 times. Of her experience she shares, "Zero gravity was even worse for my hair than humidity."

June 17

1579: Sir Francis Drake claims California for England as he anchors just north of San Francisco. He declares, "And I claim this spot right here for my great, great, great grandson. It'll be just perfect for one of the first 'In-N-Out Burger' locations!"

June 18

1960: Arnold Palmer shoots a 65 to win the U.S. Open in Denver, Colorado. To celebrate, he drinks a mixture of iced tea and lemonade, and asks the bartender, "Hey, what the hell do you call this drink?"

June 19

1897: Moe Howard of The Three Stooges is born. He immediately proceeds to slap the obstetrician right back for being a "knucklehead".

June 20

1947: Mobster Bugsy Siegel dies of natural causes. "Natural causes" in his world means that his body is "riddled with bullets and stomped on".

June 21

1834: American inventor Cyrus McCormick patents the reaping machine. At first, farmers are scared of the sharp blades on the machine, but calm down in July of 1976 when one-hit-wonder Blue Oyster Cult drops "Don't Fear the Reaper".

June 22

1633: Galileo Galilei is forced by the Pope to recant his Copernican view that the Earth orbits the Sun. 359 years later, The Vatican finally admits it was wrong in 1992, stating, "Yeah, we just figured we'd think it over for a while..."

June 23

1784: Edward Warren undertakes the first manned balloon flight in the US. Being only 13, once he landed he was grounded.

June 24

1497: John Cabot claims Eastern Canada for England, believing he has found Asia in Nova Scotia. His confusion leads to the creation of the popular "cream cheese and lox" sushi roll.

June 25

1630: The fork is introduced to American dining by John Winthrop, governor of Massachusetts. He repeatedly gets the crap beaten out of him when offering the utensil to restaurant patrons while saying, "Fork, you?"

June 26

1974: Derek Jeter is born. Lucky for his mom, it was just a short stop to the hospital.

June 27

1929: The first color TV demo is performed by Bell Laboratories in NYC. The results are inconclusive, as the guy on the screen is a white man wearing a black tuxedo.

June 28

1971: Elon Musk is born. When his mother burps him, he doesn't release gas - just electricity.

June 29

1967, 1995, 2003: Jayne Mansfield, Lana Turner, and Katherine Hepburn all die on this date. Men in heaven declare, "I feel like I died and went to Heav- oh, wait...

June 30

2010: "Scream" actress Neve Campbell divorces British actor John Light due to irreconcilable differences, including his inability to make her scream.

JULY

July 1

1997: United Kingdom returns Hong Kong and the New Territories to the People's Republic of China. Don't ask what the movers charged.

July 2

1843: According to a report in the Times Picayune of Charleston, South Carolina, during a thunderstorm an alligator fell from the sky. Fortunately it appears the beast didn't teach other gators how to fly.

July 3

1928: John Logie Baird demonstrates the first color television. He'd built his first working television set five years earlier, constructing it from - and we're not joking - an old hat box and a pair of scissors, some darning needles, a few bicycle light lenses, and a tea chest. When he dropped by the Daily Express newspaper hoping to get publicity, the editor told a staffer "For God's sake, go down to reception and get rid of a lunatic who's down there. He says he's got a machine for seeing by wireless! Watch him—he may have a razor on him."

July 4

1892: Western Samoa changes the International Date Line, so that year there were two occurrences of Monday, July 4. Two Mondays in one week - horrifying.

July 5

1994: Amazon.com is founded in Bellevue, Washington by Jeff Bezos. He offers free shipping all over the world, except to the Amazon.

July 6

2020: Kansas City Chiefs quarterback Patrick Mahomes agrees to the largest contract for an athlete in sports history, a 12-year deal worth up to $503 million. When asked why $500 million wasn't enough, he replies, "Hey, what if I have kids someday who want to go to private colleges?"

July 7

1990: The first 'Three Tenors' concert featuring Plácido Domingo, José Carreras and Luciano Pavarotti is performed in Rome. During the encore, roadies are told to find 'three tens' from the audience to bring backstage to the singers' dressing rooms.

July 8

1800: Dr. Benjamin Waterhouse gives the first cowpox vaccination in the U.S. to his son to prevent smallpox. It succeeds; and, as a bonus, the Waterhouse family never has to go shopping for milk ever again.

July 9

1964: Courtney Love is born, eventually filling a big hole in the music world. Eventually, so did Kurt Cobain.

July 10

2018: Drake surpasses The Beatles' record of most singles in the Billboard Hot 100 with seven (vs. their five) from his album "Scorpion". Paul McCartney asks his wife, "How many lads are in The Drakes, anyway?

July 11

1663: Oxford mathematician John Wallis gives the first Western lecture on Euclid's parallel postulate. Millions of fellow Brits respond with, "That's nice, but could he maybe also figure out a way to get rid of our poop besides dumping it in the streets?"

July 12

1804: Alexander Hamilton dies after being shot in a pistol duel the previous day by Aaron Burr. Historians claim that there was considerably less singing involved than most twenty first century people would think.

July 13

1772: Captain James Cook begins his second voyage aboard the Resolution to the South Seas to search for Terra Australis. He booked the same ship because of its "famous 24-hour buffet" and the free shiatsu massage coupon he'd been given on his first voyage.

July 14

1988: WYHY Radio offers a million dollars to anyone who can prove that Elvis Presley is still alive. So now we know exactly who to blame for those imitators.

July 15

1799: The Rosetta Stone is discovered by representatives of Napoleon exploring Egypt. The Egyptians loan it to the French for a 30 day trial.

July 16

1449: Kissing is banned in England to stop the Black Plague from spreading. The ban is eventually lifted when people realize that when Englanders kiss, at least they're not exposing their hideous yellow, cruddy teeth.

July 17

1070: Arnulf III the Hapless becomes Earl of Flanders. He goes on to screw up that gig, just like everything else he ever tried to do.

July 18

1936: Famous gangster "Lucky" Luciano is sentenced to 30 to 50 years in prison. Living up to his name, his sentence is commuted and he's released after only 10.

July 19

1843: The steamship SS Great Britain is launched. It's the first ocean-going craft with a screw propeller, and the largest vessel afloat in the world. The propeller is also connected to the world's largest rubber band.

July 20

1881: Sioux Indian Chief Sitting Bull surrenders to U.S. federal troops. The feds tell him to, "Stand up already - we're not bending down to put on these handcuffs."

July 21

1925: John T. Scopes found guilty of teaching evolution in the "Scopes monkey trial" in Dayton, Tennessee. Supporters of evolution worldwide go ape.

July 22

1099: First Crusade - Godfrey of Bouillon is elected the first Defender of the Holy Sepulchre of The Kingdom of Jerusalem. He immediately goes to the Holy Sepulchre kitchen and adds "little dried out cubes of chicken and beef" to several recipes.

July 23

1978: Franklin Bradshaw is murdered in Salt Lake City by his grandson Marc Schreuder at the instigation of his mother, Frances Schreuder. And you thought your family's Thanksgivings were awkward

REPLACE

July 24

1965: Bob Dylan releases "Like a Rolling Stone". He'd changed the title from "Like a Beatle", because the only rhyme he could find for that was "fetal".

July 25

1814: English engineer George Stephenson introduces his first steam locomotive, a train that would stop in various places and also offer locals a service to remove the wrinkles from their clothing.

July 26

1984: Pete Rose ties Ty Cobb with his 3,502nd single. After tying Ty, Pete treats his teammates to Thai food. But only if they wear a tie.

July 27

1586: Walter Raleigh brings the first tobacco to England from Virginia. He quickly opens a tobacco shop, beating John Luckystrike and Susan Virginiaslims to the punch.

July 28

1978: 600,000 attend the "Summer Jam" rock festival at Watkins Glen, New York, at the time the largest ever audience at a pop festival. Festival organizers admit that they "probably" should have provided more than five Port-O-Sans.

July 29

1973: Led Zeppelin has more than $200,000 in cash stolen from a safety-deposit box at the New York Hilton. Fans hardly recognize them when the band has no choice but to perform that night at Madison Square Garden completely drug-free.

July 30

1935: First Penguin Book is published, starting the paperback revolution. Authors go on to write books about igloos, polar bears, Eskimos, and many other things.

July 31

1965: Author J.K. Rowling is born. Is named a billionaire by Forbes in 2004 and changes surname to "Rowlingindough".

AUGUST

August 1

1955: First microgravity research begins. Many physicists deride the subject as lightweight.

August 2

1973: George Lucas' "American Graffiti" premieres at a film festival in Switzerland. The Swiss reaction to the movie is, as expected, neutral.

August 3

1908: Two French brothers discover the fossilized remains of man dating back 60,000 years, completely upstaging Mel Brooks

August 4

1757: American Revolution patriot Paul Revere weds Sarah Orne in Bridgewater, Massachusetts. That night, he screams from their honeymoon suite, "The newlyweds are coming! The newlyweds are coming!"

August 5

1861: Abraham Lincoln signs the first income tax into law. Or, as accountants call it, "The CPA Emancipation and Afford a Vacation Home Act".

August 6

1968: Children's author Theodor Geisel, AKA Dr. Seuss weds Audrey Stone Dimond. The next morning, she lovingly serves him breakfast in bed, consisting of...well, you know.

August 7

1820: First potatoes planted in Hawaii. In protest, Idaho farmers start planting macadamia nut trees.

August 8

1955: Fidel Castro forms the "26th of July Movement", a Cuban revolutionary organization. When asked why he does this on the 8th of August, he replies, "Because, ummh...Merry Christmas everybody!"

August 9th

1638: Jonas Bronck of Holland becomes the first European settler in the Bronx. Years later, he laments, "If my last name had only been Manhattan, I'd be a rich man today."

August 10

1904: Dutch newspaper Volk fires a popular gay journalist. The editors swear it isn't because he was gay, but is more about his name: Jacob de Cock (yes, really).

August 11

1597: Germany throws out English sales people. Citizens complain that they can't find a decent muffin anywhere.

August 12

2005: In a rare event, a tornado hits Long Island. Estimates reach hundreds of millions of dollars in damage to hairstyles and SUVs.

August 13

1948: the U.S.A. wins Olympic gold again in basketball. The losing team, France, objects to having to wear jerseys that say "Washington Generals".

August 14

1908: First beauty contest held. Occurring in England, the tie-breaker category is "most teeth".

August 15

1988: New York City declares a plan to spend over $80,000 per apartment to renovate 900 rent subsidized apartments. Contractor promises the work will be finished "any day now".

August 16

1988: IBM introduces the first artificial intelligence software. 35 years later, still no robot maid.

August 17

1953: First meeting of Narcotics Anonymous in Southern California. Widely hailed as a breakthrough in giving dealers a way to find customers.

August 18

1981: Herschel Walker, University of Georgia running back, takes out a "Lloyd's of London" insurance policy for $1 million, which seems excessive for his '79 Honda Civic.

August 19

1934: The first Soap Box Derby is held in Dayton, Ohio, giving dads and their sons a chance to finally bond by cheating together.

August 20

1619: the first African Americans in America arrive to be sold in to slavery at Point Comfort, Virginia, extablishing an American tradition of dark irony.

August 21

2018: Californian Representative Duncan Hunter indicted for using campaign funds for personal expenses including a flight for his pet rabbit. Pundits agree it's the most adorable corruption they've ever seen.

August 22

1849: The first air raid in history; Austria launches pilotless balloons against the city of Venice. Venice responds by saying "And it's not even our birthday!"

August 23

1872: First Japanese commercial ship visits San Francisco, carrying tea, or anyway that's what they told the Customs officials.

August 24

2006: The International Astronomical Union declares that Pluto is too small to be considered a planet. Pluto responds by overcompensating for its diminutive size by working out incessantly, guzzling protein shakes, and buying a new Tesla that it can't afford.

August 25

1910: Yellow Cab is founded, proving that a business can be a huge success if it just treats its customers badly enough.

August 26

1959: British Motor Cars introduces the "Mini - at only 10 feet long it has seating for 4 Brits, or 2 guys from New Jersey.

August 27

1896: Britain defeats Zanzibar in a 38-minute war, from 9:02 A.M. to 9:40 A.M., the shortest recorded war in history. Historians agree that Zanzibar folks are just not morning people.

August 28

1845: Scientific American magazine publishes its first issue with a cover article entitled, "How Charles Darwin Can Help You Get Ready For Bikini Season!"

August 29

2012: Banana Spider venom is found to be effective in relieving erectile dysfunction, providing an option for men who are cheap and very, very brave.

August 30

1146: European leaders outlaw the crossbow, intending to end war for all time. Spoiler alert - it didn't work.

August 31

1422: Henry VI becomes King of England at the age of 9 months. Attitudes towards child labor were very, very different back then.

SEPTEMBER

September 1

1752: Liberty Bell arrives in Philadelphia. The purchase price was a mere 100 pounds, but in retrospect the city should have opted for the extended warranty.

September 2

1752: the British empire - including the American colonies - switches from the Julian calendar to the Gregorian. The next day would be September 14, skipping 11 days. Landlords are ecstatic.

September 3

1939: In response to the U.K. declaring war on Germany, infamous Nazi sympathizer Unity Mitford commits the world's slowest suicide. A self-inflicted bullet lodges in her head and doesn't kill her until 1948. She just couldn't get anything right.

September 4

1842: Work on Cologne cathedral recommences after a 284-year hiatus. Contractor apologizes, claims his guys got held up on a kitchen renovation that ran long.

September 5

1698: Russian Tsar Peter the Great imposes a tax on beards. Gay men and their "girlfriends" declare the move "not fabulous."

September 6

1622: Spanish silver fleet disappears off Florida Keys. Spain's King issues first Silver Alert.

September 7

1927: Philo Farnsworth demonstrates his new invention "television," instantly giving millions of mothers babysitters that their husbands won't try to seduce.

September 8

1946: San Francisco 49ers play their first game, losing to the New York Yankees. What? The Yankees back then were even winning at football? Showoffs...

September 9

1976: The first VCR to use VHS tapes, the Victor HR-3300, is introduced by the president of JVC in Japan. Unfortunately, he leaves the videotape in the machine and now owes a late fee of $2.7 million.

September 10

1849: Edward Booth performs *Richard III* in New York as the first starring stage role by an American born actor. Edward Booth would go on to save the life of Abraham Lincoln's son, while his brother John would go on to have a more famous connection to the Lincoln family.

September 11

1883: James Cutler patents the mail chute. We imagine that one day he was in an office building, accidentally dropped an envelope down an air shaft and exclaimed "Ah, chute" .

September 12

1895: Annie Londonderry arrives in Chicago having completed the first trip around the world by a woman on a bicycle, receiving a prize of around $350K in today's dollars. That was one heck of a spin class.

September 13

1949: The Ladies Pro Golf Association of America (LPGA) forms in New York City, proving that women need an excuse to get away from their spouses on the weekend, too.

September 14

1847: US Marines enter Mexico City, inspiring the line "Halls of Montezuma". Montezuma's been getting his revenge ever since.

September 15

1821: Guatemala declares independence from Spain. To this day, Spain is not convinced at all when Guatemala says, "It wasn't you, it was me".

September 16

1873: German troops leave France. Spoiler alert- they'd be back . They're the herpes of armies.

September 17

1683: Dutch scientist Antonie van Leeuwenhoek is the first to report the existence of bacteria. Mrs. van Leeuwenhoek declares, "You try to raise three kids and keep this place spotless!"

September 18

1891: Harriet Maxwell Converse is the first white woman to become an Indian chief, and we're just as confused as you are.

September 19

335: Dalmatius is raised to the rank of Caesar. He spends his entire reign lobbying, in vain, to have a salad named after his original name.

September 20

1870: Mayor William "Boss" Tweed is accused of robbing the New York City Treasury. As a defense he asks, "Why else would anyone go into politics?"

September 21

1776: Five days after the British arrive in New York a quarter of the city burns to the ground. Worst Airbnb guests ever.

September 22

1943: British dwarf submarines attack German battleship Tirpitz, but the British Navy swears it was just that all the cold water caused shrinkage.

September 23

1952: First PPV sports event. 21 year old Don King hears about it and says "Hmmmm..."

September 24

1869: Wall Street has its first of what would eventually be many Black Fridays. Only the rich could manage to hate Fridays.

September 25

1861: Secretary of U.S. Navy authorizes enlistment of slaves. Navy enlisted vets know the feeling.

September 26

1772: New Jersey passes a bill requiring a license to practice medicine. Another example of big government stifling entrepreneurs.

September 27

1908: The first Ford Model T rolls off the assembly line. No word on whether the buyer sprang for the AC or glossy red calipers.

September 28

1785: Napoleon Bonaparte, who would go on to be hailed as one of the most brilliant battle strategists of all time, graduates from the Elite École Militaire in Paris forty second out of a class of fifty one. So if your kid gets lousy grades don't despair, someday he or she might end up exiled to a tiny island.

September 29

1943: Italian Marshal Pietro Badoglio signs an armistice with the Allies. Apparently "armistice" in Italian means, "General Eisehower, please stop stomping on our balls!"

September 30

1960: The Flintstones premieres on ABC. Jackie Gleason and Art Carney immediately call their lawyers asking if it's possible to sue a cartoon character.

OCTOBER

October 1

2019: A law allowing teachers to carry guns in schools comes into effect in Florida. Suddenly, hundreds of teachers are seen squinting while breathily saying, "Go ahead, make my daycare."

October 2

1942: Jazz great Louis Armstrong divorces Alpha Smith. Louis was looking for a much beta relationship.

October 3

1899: J.S. Thurman patents a motor-driven vacuum cleaner. He decides to reject the advertising slogan: "This product really sucks!"

October 4

1994: Sting's financial manager Keith Moore is charged with theft after it is discovered that he pilfered nearly 10 million dollars from the rock star. In other words, he got stung in a sting for stealing from Sting.

October 5

1902: McDonald's founder Ray Croc is born. He was a very tiny preemie; only a quarter pounder.

October 6

1783: Benjamin Hanks patents a self-winding clock. That guy was no slouch; a real self-starter.

October 7

1931: Nobel Peace Prize winner Desmond Tutu is born. Though he lived until 2021, he was really hoping to make it to twenty twenty two two.

October 8

1967: South American guerilla leader Che Guevara is captured by the Bolivian Army and charged with treason and intent to make the beret a fashion trend.

October 9

1865: The first US underground pipeline for carrying oil is laid in Pennsylvania. Sadly, because oil is highly flammable, it could not enjoy a cigarette afterward.

October 10

1959: "Happy Town" closes at the 84th Street Theater in Manhattan after just five performances. The town itself may be happy, but the investors and ticket buying theatergoers are pissed as hell.

October 11

1975: "Saturday Night Live" premieres on NBC with host George Carlin. Ruthless critics immediately say, "It used to be much better. Like before it was even on."

October 12

1935: Luciano Pavarotti is born in Modena, Italy. When he starts crying, his mother demands 900 lira from everyone in the delivery room, claiming it's his "first concert".

October 13

1988: The Shroud of Turin, revered by many Christians as Christ's burial cloth, is shown by carbon-dating tests to be a fake. Another tip-off is the tag that reads "Dry Clean Only."

October 14

1957: The Everly Brothers' single "Wake Up Little Susie" reaches #1. It was reportedly inspired by Susie's night of debauchery with both brothers, and the frantic attempts to revive her the following morning so she could make them pancakes.

October 15

1886: Modest Mussorgsky's musical fantasy *Night on Bald Mountain* premieres in St. Petersburg, Russia. His sequel piece debuts in Great Neck, New York in 1889, and was entitled, *An Enchanted Afternoon at the Hair Club for Men.*

October 16

1884: The London Prison for Debtors closes. They just couldn't meet their overhead.

October 17

1938: Daredevil Evel Knievel is born. He goes on to make himself and countless orthopedic surgeons multimillionaires.

October 18

1931: Thomas Edison, inventor of the electric light bulb, among many other things, dies at age 84. New York Post headline: "It's Lights Out For Edison!"

October 19

1216: King John of England dies and is succeeded by his nine-year-old son Henry. King Henry's first royal decree is for a million-billion-gazillion gallons of ice cream to be sent to his castle. Oh, and a pony

October 20

1774: The American Continental Congress orders "discouragement of entertainment". They go on to clarify that it's still perfectly alright to purchase those tickets to see Carrot Top.

October 21

1879: Thomas Edison invents a commercially practical incandescent light. This invention rocks the world of illustration, as artists would no longer draw a lit candle over the head of someone having an idea.

October 22

1962: U.S. President John F. Kennedy imposes a naval blockade on Cuba, beginning the missile crisis. And of much more concern to American steakhouse aficionados, a Cuban cigar crisis.

October 23

42 BC: Roman Republican civil wars: Brutus' army is decisively defeated by Mark Antony and Octavian. Brutus commits suicide. Finally, Popeye can eat his damn spinach and enjoy a night at home with Olive Oyl in peace.

October 24

2017: Fats Domino dies, leaving the title of "Best Overweight African-American World-Class Musician with a Parlor Game Surname" to Chubby Checker.

October 25

2015: Singer Jason Mraz weds his girlfriend Christina Carano. Christina immediately makes it clear to Jason that now that he is married, he must be completely faithful to her and not get any "More Azz" on the side.

October 26

1881: Cowboys Tom and Frank McLaurey get killed in the "Shootout at the O.K. Corral". Surviving relatives push for a name change to the "Not Really O.K. As Far As Our Family Is Concerned" Corral.

October 27

1925: Water skis are patented by Fred Waller. The patent stated simply, "Skis, but... now hear me out... for water."

October 28

1538: The first university in the New World, the Universidad Santo Tomás de Aquino, is established on Hispaniola. Graduates of universities in the Old World immediately try to transfer credits.

October 29

1929: The Wall Street Stock Market crash, known as "Black Tuesday," occurs, triggering the Great Depression. While formerly wealthy, now-bankrupt New Yorkers can no longer afford to drive to New England to watch the Autumn leaves fall from the trees, they can at least walk downtown and watch stockbrokers fall from Wall Street windows.

October 30

1917: British government gives final approval to Balfour Declaration. Catcher replies, "You're blind! It was right down the pipe, and why are we playing baseball in England, anyhow?!"

October 31

1918: The Spanish Flu kills 21,000 people in the U.S. in a single week. President Woodrow Wilson declares, "We are not a vengeful nation. I have no plans whatsoever to unleash the American Flu on Spain."

November

November 1

1896: The first bare-breasted woman appears in National Geographic Magazine. Coincidentally, this also marks the first appearance of teenage boys insisting on having locks on their bedroom doors.

November 2

2006: Rod Stewart (58) and model Rachel Hunter (33) divorce after he doesn't like her answer to his question, "Do Ya Think I'm Sexy?"

November 3

1906: International Radiotelegraph Conference in Berlin selects "SOS" as the worldwide standard for help. They also select it "for those grimy, greasy, impossible to clean pots and pans."

November 4

1841: First wagon train arrives in California. When it gets to the Beverly Hills Hotel, a valet parking kid leaves it right out front, calling it, "kick ass, freakin' awesome!"

November 5

1605: Conspirator Guy Fawkes attempts to blow up King James I and the British Parliament. Celebrated with fireworks ever since as Guy Fawkes Day. Hence the expression when a celebrator accidentally blows off a few fingers, "Damn, I really Fawked up!"

November 6

1918: Mahatma Gandhi arrested for leading Indian miners' march in South Africa. He promises, from that day on, to organize protests only with people age 18 and over.

November 7

2020: Joe Biden declared the winner of the U.S. Presidential race over Donald Trump, leading to the sudden mysterious disappearance of 150 million red baseball caps throughout the country.

November 8

1602: The Bodleian Library at Oxford University opens. It remains completely empty for three months, because the person announcing the opening keeps getting shushed by the librarian.

November 9

1494: Piero the Unfortunate of the de' Medici family, ruler of Florence, loses his power and flees the state. To drown his sorrow he hits a casino in Venice to play some baccarat and quickly goes "underwater", living up to his name.

November 10

1940: Walt Disney begins serving as an informer to the FBI; his job is to report back information on Hollywood subversives. He immediately proceeds to rat on "subversives" Mr. Sixflags, Mrs. Knott'sberry, and Mr. Universal.

November 11

1675: German mathematician Gottfried Wilhelm Leibniz demonstrates integral calculus for the first time to find the area under the graph of y = f(x) function. Unbeknownst to him, on that day he also launches the now multi-million dollar math tutoring industry.

November 12

1927: Leon Trotsky is expelled from the Soviet Communist Party after complaining that his annual Party dues were "way too expensive", essentially amounting to Capitalism.

November 13

1577: Francis Drake sets sail from England on a circumnavigation of the world. His motivation was to find deli and bodega owners willing to give him shelf space to sell his Devil Dogs, Yankee Doodles, Funny Bones, and Ring Dings.

November 14

1834: Future mathematical physicist William Thomson enters Glasgow University at the age of 10. He is torn between majoring in quantum physics or ringolevio.

November 15

1904: King C. Gillette patents the Gillette razor blade. He calls his competitor's blade "a total piece of Schick."

November 16

1519: City of Havana moves to a new location to avoid mosquito infestations.

On November 17, 1519, the mosquitos decide to move to the new place, too.

November 17

2018: Danny DeVito Day is celebrated in Asbury Park, NJ. Ironically, they don't pick December 21, which is the shortest day of the year.

November 18

1307: William Tell shoots an apple off his son's head. Well, the son we all know about. He gets irate when you bring up the other two, may they rest in peace…

November 19

1895: American inventor Frederick E. Blaisdell patents the pencil. A year earlier, his mother had nagged him to, "Get the lead out of your pants and invent something already!"

November 20

1521: Arabs attribute shortage of water in Jerusalem to Jews making wine. Jews tell them to "Stop with the whining already. Always with the whining."

November 21

1837: Thomas Morris of Australia skips rope 22,806 times. It was actually more, but while he was skipping the guy who was keeping count died of old age.

November 22

1794: Strasbourg Alsace-Lorraine prohibits circumcision and wearing of beards. So it was 0-for-2 that day for the mohels.

November 23

1556: King Philip II confers with Dutch financial experts. Their advice, "Don't let your great, great, great, grandson's mother throw away his Mantle rookie card."

November 24

1993: Brady bill passes, establishing 5-day waiting period for U.S. handgun sales. Frustrated prospective purchasers of handguns ask if there's any waiting period to buy bazookas, machetes, or dynamite.

November 25

1783: Britain evacuates New York City, its last military position in the United States. When asked why they left New York for last, their leader says, "We figured we'd catch a Broadway show, hit Macy's, and maybe grab a pastrami sandwich over at Katz's before we go home."

November 26

1716: First lion exhibited in America in Boston. Toddlers start crying and screaming at their parents, "You call this a zoo? Where's the monkey house? I have to make a doody!"

November 27

1911: Audience throws vegetables at actors for the first recorded time in the U.S. The confused entertainers conclude that they're probably tips and start yelling out the names of their favorite foods.

November 28

1942: The U.S. government begins the rationing of coffee. Enraged citizens want to protest the mandate, but are just too damn tired to do anything.

November 29

1963: The Warren Commission is established to investigate the assassination of President John F. Kennedy. The most notable conclusion gleaned from ten months of exhaustive investigation? Next time, leave the top up.

November 30

2017: The world's longest recorded rainbow, 8 hours and 58 minutes, is seen in the Yangmingshan mountain range of Taipei. The following day, Taipei chiropractors strike it rich by adjusting 245,671 stiff necks.

DECEMBER

December 1

1921: The first U.S. helium-filled dirigible makes its maiden voyage. Crew and passengers on the vessel give a rousing and extremely high-pitched "Hurrah!"

December 2

1982: Doctors at the University of Utah Medical Center perform the first implant of a permanent artificial heart. The patient then rejoins his companions the Scarecrow and Cowardly Lion and returns to Oz.

December 3

1984: Union Carbide pesticide plant leaks 45 tons of methyl isocyanate and other toxic compounds in Bhopal, India, killing 2,259. Survivors in Bophal say, "Finally! A family picnic without any bugs, whatsoever!"

December 4

1154: Pope Adrian IV becomes the only Englishman to be elected pontiff. Controversy soon follows as the sacramental wine and host are replaced with warm beer and fish & chips.

December 5

1868: First American bicycle college opens in New York. Course offerings include, "How to Get Back Your Stolen Bike When You See it at a Flea Market" and "How to Not Look Like a Dork on a Bicycle Built for Two".

December 6

1790: The U.S. Congress moves from New York City to Philadelphia, Pennsylvania. Congress spokesman: "Look, that Manhattan rent was just killing us. I mean, fifteen bucks a month for an unfurnished meeting room with cockroaches?"

December 7

1940: Americans are unaware that this will be the last December seventh that they won't have to listen to FDR's insufferable "Day of Infamy" speech.

December 8

1966: The United States and the USSR sign a treaty to prohibit nuclear weapons in outer space. The Earth? That's another question...

December 9

1956: NBA star Bill Russell (22) weds college sweetheart Rose Swisher. SWISH!

December 10

1901: First Nobel Prize in physics is awarded to Wilhelm Roentgen for the x-ray. He tells the Nobel committee, "But there is no Nobel Prize for physics; it just doesn't exist. Really, guys, I can see right through you."

December 11

2014: Surgeons in South Africa perform the world's first penis transplant. They claim that they would have done a testicles transplant too, but, "Unfortunately, we just didn't have the balls to do it."

December 12

1957: Jerry Lee Lewis (21) weds his cousin Myra Gale Brown (13) while still married to his second wife. People debate over what's worse: committing adultery, marrying one's cousin, having relations with a 13-year old, or having to listen to Jerry Lee bang on that piano.

December 13

1961: Painter Grandma Moses dies at 101. Relatives are beside themselves: "Why? Why? Just nine short years from 110..."

December 14

1947: NASCAR is founded in Daytona Beach, Florida. Audience of right-wingers come to racetrack to see only left turns.

December 15

1840: Napoleon Bonaparte receives a French state funeral in Paris nineteen years after his death. And you'd thought the reason France stinks is because they don't use deodorant.

December 16

1773: Boston Tea Party - Sons of Liberty protesters throw tea shipments into Boston harbor apparently in protest against the British imposed tax on tea. Truth be told, it was because the tea was way past its expiration date.

December 17

1903: The Wright brothers make the first sustained motorized aircraft flight, piloted by Orville at Kitty Hawk, North Carolina. For whatever reason, Orville gets to do all the fun stuff. Wilbur, on the other hand, has to give the plane a push start, wash it after the flight, and then put it back in the hangar.

December 18

2019: The U.S. House of Representatives votes to impeach President Donald Trump for abuse of power, obstruction of Congress, and for having hair unbefitting of his office.

December 19

2010: Fans witness "The Miracle at the New Meadowlands", with the Philadelphia Eagles beating the New York Giants after trailing by 21 points with just eight minutes to go. Fans who left the game early experienced an even bigger miracle: getting out of the stadium parking lot in under 45 minutes.

December 20

1937: Chicago Black Hawks left wing Paul Thompson becomes first player in NHL history to score a goal against his own brother. Their parents are in the stands with dad cheering and mom booing. They divorce the next day.

December 21

401: St. Innocent I begins his reign as Catholic Pope. He accomplishes absolutely nothing during his entire time as Pope; except for repeating, "I swear I didn't do it. I wasn't even in town! Ask anybody!"

December 22

1852: First Chinese theater in the U.S, the Celestial John, opens in San Francisco. An hour after the theatergoers watch the movie, they get an irresistible yen to watch another one.

December 23

1888: Vincent van Gogh cuts off his left ear with a razor after arguing with fellow painter Paul Gauguin. He then sends the ear to a prostitute for safe keeping. After that, Vincent goes on to have an otherwise uneventful day.

December 24

1906: Reginald Fessenden transmits the first radio broadcast; consisting of a poetry reading, a violin solo, and a speech. The first caller into the radio station actually did guess the "Phrase That Pays", which was "Watson, Come here I need you."

December 25

1 AD: First Christmas. Kids pissed off that there are no presents. Parents respond, "How were we supposed to know? And how did that fat guy get in here? Get off his lap!"

December 26

1966: The Exorcist becomes the first horror film to be nominated for Best Picture. It features the most talked about head turning in cinema history until 2022 when Will Smith slaps Chris Rock.

December 27

1939: Between 20,000 and 40,000 die in a magnitude 8 earthquake in Erzincam, Turkey. Those estimates are so far apart because the first guy keeping count died in the earthquake, and the second guy had to start from scratch.

December 28

1950: Author John Steinbeck weds actress Elaine Anderson. Three men serve as ushers. And three mice.

December 29

1845: Texas admitted as the 28th state of the Union. Texas immediately complains: "You should go by size. We're actually the first state!"

December 30

1955: Actor Gregory Peck divorces Greta Kukkonen, a real estate agent. She keeps the house: "A 5,750 sf, 5 BR, 4.5 bath colonial with unequaled lake view, totally renovated kitchen with gas cooking, black quartz countertops and a "chef's dream" center island..."

December 31

1775: Battle of Quebec in the American Revolutionary War is fought. The loser is forced to keep all of Canada.

ABOUT THE AUTHORS

Michael Morse is a headlining comedian, comedy writer, and illustrator. His credits include *The Tonight Show*, *The Howard Stern Show*, and the hit podcast, *The Uncle Rico Show*. He still can't believe that a guy as accomplished as he is, was involved in a project with the three individuals described below.

Neil Berliner is a comedy writer and comedian with credits on *The Comedy Central Roasts*, *The Friars Club Roasts*, *The Howard Stern Show*, *The New York Times*, and *MAD Magazine*. He is also a practicing medical doctor, but only from Mondays to Wednesdays, 10 AM to 1:15 PM Eastern time.

Joey Novick is a comedian who has opened for people like Jerry Seinfeld, Robert Klein, and Chris Rock. He is also an entertainment attorney and an elected official in New Jersey. Joey came up with the idea for this book, which he incessantly reminded the other three authors of at every single writers meeting they held throughout 2022.

Ron Beau Phillips is an actor, comedian, and IT professional who once worked at NASA. He is the most interesting of the four authors here. For instance, although never arrested, he has been detained by police at gunpoint on five different occasions, two of them while naked (Ron, not the police) . He's opened for Doug Stanhope. His comedy credentials are not as strong as those of the above three authors, so we decided to put his bio last, hoping that nobody would be reading at this point.